1 MONTH OF
FREE
READING

at

www.ForgottenBooks.com

By purchasing this book you are eligible for one month membership to ForgottenBooks.com, giving you unlimited access to our entire collection of over 1,000,000 titles via our web site and mobile apps.

To claim your free month visit:

www.forgottenbooks.com/free777923

ISBN 978-0-428-80698-9
PIBN 10777923

THE INFLUENCE OF COMMERCE UPON CHRISTIANITY.

A PRIZE ESSAY,

READ IN THE THEATRE, OXFORD,

JUNE 28, 1854.

BY

WILLIAM HENRY FREMANTLE, B. A.

BALL. COLL.

OXFORD:

T. AND G. SHRIMPTON.

M DCCC LIV.

THE INFLUENCE OF COMMERCE
UPON CHRISTIANITY.

THERE is a great difference between Christianity in itself, and Christianity as it has been in the world. The one is perfect and complete, eternal and immutable, an emanation from God himself, possessed of the attributes of its Author, and to be known so far and in the same manner as He is known. The other is modified and fluctuating, even where the actual corresponds nearest to the ideal; and as we trace it in the lower sphere of its operation, it is subjected to conditions and applications various as the characters of mankind, and becomes only one of the many forces which impel the machine of society—one of the elements which make up the complex organization of human nature. Now we have in this lower sphere a thousand influences and agencies, acting and reacting one upon another. The difference between all these forces and Christianity is that the former are of human origin, in themselves fluctuating and varying, the latter has a higher origin and a higher existence of its own : *they* are of the earth and spring from beneath, *it* comes down from above. These forces, therefore, can never reach into the upper region—the region of absolute truth ; but they have a sphere of their own in which the absolute truth can be to a certain extent apprehended ; and this is the sphere of history and historical investigation. In looking back upon the past and recounting what has happened, we see Christianity not in its absolute form, but as it appeared to men—as it was influenced by or had influence upon their thoughts and their actio͏
In considering, therefore, the influence of commerce up

Christianity, we are completely cut off from any investigation of the essence of Christianity, and are only to inquire what has been the actual result where these two forces have been brought in contact.

Before, however, we proceed to the direct inquiry, it may be well to examine the direction in which these forces generally influence the world, and the points which they have in common. And first we must determine what sphere we are to assign to commerce, and in how wide a sense we are to use the word.

In its most general sense, then, commerce is the interchange of commodities: and in this all men are alike engaged. It is impossible for men to live together in society without such dealings continually going forward, and the origin of political life has been traced to the necessity of them. Hence, in a sense, all men are commercial, for all men make exchanges: commerce is the primary element of a civilized life—that without which civilization cannot exist. If we could imagine a tribe of savages passing out of a nomad state and settling down into fixed habitations, one of the first proceedings would be the subdivision of labour and the assignation of trades to particular individuals. No longer would each man provide himself with food from the flesh and milk of his own cattle, or with raiment from their skins; but, as the arts of life became known, the weaver and the farmer and the cobbler would provide the produce of his own art for others beside himself. Hence trade is the substratum of civilization, that which underlies all higher efforts. But in the advanced stages of civilization, when the human race has attained a higher state, this substratum is no longer necessarily the most important element; other principles may arise of greater value. Commerce may, it is true, continually increase, and be the chief characteristic of a highly civilized state, as is the case with the United States; but it is by no means so with the highly cultivated nations of the Old World, France and Germany and Italy. In this more advanced stage, the commerce necessary for common civilization is assumed—it is implied in the fact that these nations are civilized: and the distinction of commercial and non-commercial nations refers not to this low and more limited kind of trade, but to commerce in its grander and more extensive operations. The spirit, however, is in all cases the same; and it is well to remember, when we speak of commercial classes and commercial countries that no class and no country is altogether without commerce or uninfluenced by the commercial spirit.

We may learn then that commerce influences mankind from beneath; it belongs in the first instance to their material progress. Christianity on the contrary, comes down from above, and influences in the first instance the moral and intellectual progress. The one influences the soul through the body; the other directs the body through the soul: and their influences meet in that sphere of moral and social existence, on which are brought to bear all the converging principles of the material and intellectual world. In that middle sphere of social life, sentiments and opinions are produced by causes of many different kinds; these principles, which have nothing in common, which belong to separate fields of interest, may bear fruit in the same direction; and persons with totally different views of life may unite in one and the same opinion upon a thousand matters even of great importance. Thus it is that the spirit of commerce and that of Christianity unite in many of the sentiments and views which result from them.

Of these the most important is a love of peace. The spirit of commerce, having regard to the security and profitableness of trade is full of the warmest feelings of antipathy to war: it needs but a fair field; it desires to molest nobody: it requires but the open sea and the open highway, clear from all obstructions, unmolested by foes, where its harmless inoffensive energy may expatiate. Whatever may be the selfishness of individual traders, the general interests of this great agency are identical with those of mankind in general, and the watchword of commerce as well as of Christianity is Peace on Earth, good will towards men.

It is, moreover, a pursuit which is emphatically universal. It is connected with the first and most necessary requirements of man, as man, and belongs not to any particular countries, but to the world. It gives therefore a bond altogether independent of class or language or nationality: the merchant has to compete as much with his own countrymen as with foreigners, and feels himself as closely allied to those with whom he trades as to those among whom he lives. It insists upon the great doctrine that man is not independent of man, but, in the widest sense, that the ends of the earth are connected one with another, and nations and countries rely upon one another for mutual support.

> 'Tis thus reciprocating each with each
> Alternately the nations learn and teach,
> While Providence enjoins to every soul
> An union with the vast terraqueous whole.[1]

Such a bond as this, when once felt is by no means one which can easily be dispensed with : commerce is not only world wide in its extension, it is also continually becoming deeper in its influence. It is a tree whose roots are ever silently growing—a cord whose ends unravelled are twined round the heart of nations and amid the intricate relations of society; till at length to sever the bond would be to abolish the principle of gravitation, to hurl the nations from their appointed orbits, to reduce the moral unverse to a chaotic void, in which isolated atoms and particles move listlessly without order or law. When the corn trade with Alexandria was interrupted, Rome was starved; were the cotton trade with America cut off, whole classes in England would be reduced to poverty; and a failure in the tea-crop in China would be felt by every individual in England. Again, the effect of commerce is to level and to equalize: it starts with the fundamental maxim that all men are

---

[1] Cowper's Charity.

equal : and is in its essence opposed to all exclusive systems of caste or feudalism, to all institutions which give privileges to a single class, and all measures of government which favour monopoly and regard the interest of individuals rather than that of the whole community. In all these points it harmonizes with Christianity—a religion which teaches that every man look[1] not on his own things but also on the things of others—which tell us that men are bound together as brethren, not because they live in the same country or speak the same language ; but because they are children of the same Father, subjects of the same Lord ; which asserts that in[2] Jesus Christ there is neither Jew nor Greek, neither bond nor free ; and which brings Felix in his palace and Paul in his dungeon to stand on an equal footing before the same tribunal.

But, above all, both the elements of which we are treating, will stand the test of truth and reality and permanence. In our more enthusiastic moments, we are apt to paint to ourselves a glowing ideal picture of that high state of social progress to which, as we fain would trust, the world is tending, a golden age of human society, a millennium of regenerated existence. In that picture which the imagination draws, but which is not the less true because as yet it has no outward manifestation, and the way that leads to it appears long and difficult, the most prominent characteristic features are piety, peace and liberty. In that happy ideal, war and bloodshed, contention and variance find no place ; and with them vanish military glory, and ambition and rivalry whether of war or of politics. But when the intrigues of diplomacy and the feats of arms are gone, and when the mighty deeds and fantastic virtues of chivalry are put aside, as vain and shadowy forms, gloomy and grand, but now grown useless and even monstrous ; the genius of commerce flourishes and is welcomed, ministering to the wants of man, and driving far the approaches of

[1] Phil. ii. 4. [2] Gal. iii. 28.

poverty, and satisfying all the requirements of an ennobled and elegant civilization.[1]

But it is time to hasten from ideals to actuals—from the truth of abstraction to the truth of history, and inquire not what is the eventual destination of the two great influences which we are considering, but what has actually been their bearing one on the other. This inquiry includes two distinct matters of investigation, the one a question about events, the other about tendencies.

Firstly, in what way and in what places has commerce diffused Christianity?

Secondly, in what manner and to what extent has commerce affected the doctrines and practice of Christianity?

I. The fiction of Plato,[2] which attributes the formation of his commonwealth to the necessity of commerce between man and man, serves at any rate to show the primary importance of this element, and seems to give a sanction to the purely rational and utilitarian view of the world, which looks upon man as working upwards from the material to the intellectual, and furnishing himself with material appliances as his first and most necessary business. But, however this may be, it is sufficient for our present purpose to know that commerce was in the world antecedent to Christianity, and that the divine element came in when the ground was already occupied by the human. We cannot but regard this as a preparation of the ground for the sowing of the seed, and admit that industrial pursuits have made ready the way for the advance of Christianity. And, as a fact, we find that the course of Christian missions has almost always lain along the roads marked out by trade. In the first age of the propagation of Christianity, we find communities of Jews settled for commercial purposes in all

---

[1] See Cowper's Winter Walk at Noon.
  The looms of Ormus and the mines of Ind
  And Saba's spicy groves pay tribute there.

[2] Plato's Republic, B. II. See also Arist. Eth. Nic. B. v. 8, 11, ἡ χρεία πάντα συνέχει.

parts of the Roman empire ;' we find that empire, including within itself the whole civilized world, united by the bonds of a single government, and thus affording the means of intercommunication to all the countries under its dominion; nor was there any bond except those of political power and of law which bound the provinces together more firmly than that of commerce. The roads which were laid down wherever the Roman had conquered gave facilities for intercourse unknown before; and the abolition of piracy allowed free commerce by sea throughout the Mediterranean, now become a Roman lake. Though the Romans were not, properly speaking,[2] a commercial nation, yet their city had become the great emporium of trade, the centre light of the commercial world, compared with which the ancient seats of trade, Carthage and Tyre and Ephesus and Corinth, which had been suns in their own systems, now seemed but stars of inferior magnitude. Not only had the Archipelago, Alexandria, and the Black Sea become the purveyors of the metropolis in wine and corn and fish for the common uses of life; but the luxury of Italy attracted the choicest productions of the more remote countries into her bosom, and drew pearls and silks from the Euphrates and amber from the Baltic. The vessel which brought St. Paul to Rome was an Alexandrian corn-ship, and the voyage to Spain which he so long meditated was doubtless designed to be performed in one of the many merchant vessels which traded for wool between Cadiz and Puteoli : [3]Selencia the port of Antioch was the scene of the first embarkation of missionaries to the heathen, and Corinth and Ephesus soon became the centres for the diffusion of Christianity,[2] as they before had been of trade. And in truth had it not been for this disposition of events, which rendered all parts of the known world accessible, we find it difficult to conceive how

---

[1] The assemblage at the day of Pentecost included men from Libya, Egypt, Arabia, Persia, Mesopotamia, Asia Minor and Rome.

[2] Conybeare and Howson—Life and Epistles of St. Paul. Chapters 20, 23.

[3] Acts 13, v. 4.

B

the knowledge of the truth could have been communicated. What would have been the condition of the Apostles had the Jewish nation at the time of our Saviour's ascension been an isolated portion of the human race, without connection with the civilized world ? With their ignorance of other lands and other manners, their strong Jewish prejudices, their antipathy to foreigners, they would have been inclined to limit their efforts to their own countrymen ; and that light which, by the assistance of free commercial intercourse has illumined the world, might for ages, as far as we can judge, have remained hid in a corner, the possession of a single race ;—the desire of all nations might still have remained unsatisfied.

Thus did commerce at first give a medium for the diffusion of Christianity and enable the true religion to be planted, even in the Apostolic age, almost throughout the Roman empire.[1]   In later times we have the same connection constantly brought before us, commerce making plain the way, smoothing asperities, removing obstacles, pioneering for the march of the armies of the truth.   The existence of commerce in any high degree denotes peace as reigning at home, and a spirit of energy to carry it on beyond the confines of a single country ; it denotes, further, amity and reciprocity of feeling between those who trade together ; it tends to the discovery of new countries, to the acquisition of new languages, and generally to the promotion of friendly intercourse throughout the world.   All these are in the highest degree calculated to aid both materially and morally the cause of missions ; for not only do the material facilities given by ships and caravans and the necessary protection afforded to these by the political powers to which they belong give greater security to the missionary ; but also the kindly feeling induced by commercial interests has a moral influence over the minds of those who engage in it.   Thus the opening of the trade with the East Indies by the Cape of Good Hope in the 16th century

---

[1] Grant's Bampton Lectures, Lect. 4.

and the gold-seeking settlements of the Spaniards in
America gave occasion for the missionary enterprises of
the Jesuits,[1] and disposed the nations of China and India
and the savages of Paraguay to listen to their instructions;
nor were the Dutch[2] and British and Danish protestants who
inherited the trade in those countries unmindful of similar
efforts: the zeal of Christian missions in connection with the
extension of trade did not die away even in the deadest period
of our religious history; and the present century has beheld
at one and the same moment the great commercial schemes
which have drawn all ends of the world together, and
some of the most vigorous and successful efforts in the
cause of Christian missions which the world has ever witnessed.

But not only does commerce aid the extension of Christianity; Christianity has scarcely ever been extended beyond
the limits marked out by commerce. We have observed
how rapidly in the first age, Christianity was planted
throughout the Roman Empire; we may now further add
that during four centuries at least it was confined to the
Roman Empire. It rolled on rapidly and successfully till
it reached the limits of commerce and civilization; but
there it stayed its course, and the energy which had hitherto
borne it forward in an outward direction was now turned
back with intensive force into its own bosom. The ground[3]
which was occupied in the Apostolic age was the same in
extent as that which was covered at the time of Constan-
tine; but the little sparks of light which had glimmered

---

[1] Vid. Grant's Bampton Lectures. Smyth's Lect. on Mod. Hist. Lect. 21.—
Robertson's Hist. of America.

[2] The Dutch had missions in the 16th century in Ceylon, Ambryna, Java,
and Formosa. The king of Denmark sent a mission to the coast of Coroma-
del in 1706, which flourished during the whole of the last century under the
auspices of the Christian Knowledge Society and the illustrous names of Zieg-
enbulg, Schwartz and Kohlhoff, and has been the parent of some of the brightest successes of the present time at Tinnurlly and other places in the Madras
presidency. In America Cromwell encouraged missions, as later did Boyle,
from whose efforts the S. P. G. was founded.

[3] See Grant's Bampton Lectures, Lecture 4.

at first in the wide realm of darkness had combined into a
steady and connected glow; the cords which had been
loosely laid had become knotted into a net which encom-
passed and held fast the empire. In this case Christianity
had been pent up, but in no narrow bounds, and it had
lived and flourished and become intensified. The fact, however, remains that it stayed its outward and extensive course
where it came in contact with barbarism and with fields
which were shut to commerce. The same general remark
applies throughout the history of missions; they have seldom deviated from the beaten track of commercial enterprise; still more seldom gone beyond its range. It is true
there are exceptions; and it by no means holds good that
Christianity has been most vigorously pushed forward
wherever the most extensive trade has flourished. The
efforts of missions have been regulated by no such precise
and accurate rule. Religious zeal[1] is an element exceed-
ingly fluctuating and eccentric in its character, at one time
almost disappearing from the moral world, at another pro-
ducing the grandest results; it has worked by impulse and
enthusiasm, not by calm and sustained effort. Hence, there
have been times when the church aroused from her slum-
ber has pressed forward her outposts beyond the pale of civilization and burst through all fetters of mere prudential
considerations, and leaving behind the confines of the civilized world and the protection of civilized power, has in-
vaded the very centre of the reign of heathendom and barbarism. There were missions to the Abyssinians and the
tribes of Arabia in the very earliest ages, and churches
established by the Nestorians in India and even in China.
The missionaries of the middle age met barbarism and
savage life in the woods of Germany and the fiords of Nor-

---

[1] I desire to guard against even the appearance of speaking lightly of religious feeling. In such an enquiry as the present one must take the pheno-
mena as they occur in history, without constantly referring back to their
causes; and hence we speak of religious energy merely in its human aspect,
though if the cause be asked for we must ascribe it unhesitatingly to the work
of the Spirit of God.

way: the Jesuits outran commercial enterprise in China and Japan;[1] and in our own day we have seen the islands of the Pacific evangelized almost as soon as they became known;[2] we have seen the missionary zeal planting itself where commerce ventured not among the savage tribes of New Zealand, and defying even common discretion in the ill-fated Patagonian mission[3]

But these exceptions to the general rule when more closely examined only add strength to the intimate connection of Christianity with commerce and national civilization. For in most of these cases it has been the commerce of a Christian country which has by its renown induced a favourable acceptance of the missions. The kings of barbarian nations' in the fall of the Roman Empire, and the tribes of Northern Europe in the succeeding ages, like the South Sea Islanders[4] in the present century, were struck with the benefits of material civilization and respected its possessors. Hence they were disposed to listen to the preachers of the Christian religion as to men who were better informed and knew more than themselves; and who, as they were able to teach them the things of this life might be supposed to know also the things of the life to come. In these cases civilization has been a powerful advocate for the truth, and where Christianity has once been introduced it has been its supporter and strengthener. Indeed it is impossible for Christianity long to hold its ground without such supports: it claims them and by its precepts enjoins their establishment. The state of savage life is as much opposed to Christianity as it is to commerce and civilization. The first law given to fallen man tells him that in the sweat of his face he shall eat his bread: and throughout the Scripture the doctrine is proclaimed: If a man will not work neither shall he eat.[4] Now the life of

---

[1] Grant's Bampton Lectures, Lect. 4.

[2] Williams's Missionary Enterprises in the South Seas; also an article in the Quarterly Review of Jan. 1854, called "The Missions in Polynesia."

[3] See "Hope Deferred not Lost," by G. O. Despard.

[4] Prov. vi. 6. 2 Thess. iii. 7-10. Eph. iv. 28. Tit. iii. 14. Acts xviii. 2.

a savage is a direct contradiction to this universal
law: he refuses to till the ground, to apply himself to
labour, or in any way to subdue the earth which is
given for the use of man: he announces himself a vagabond
upon the earth, an outcast from civilization, a scorner of
the arts of peace and the restraints of social life. The
Scriptures on the other hand insist upon,—they even presume—society and law and order,[1] and by constant precept
enjoin on us labour and patient industry ; nor is there any
more remarkable characteristic of a Christian nation, as
contrasted with a tribe of savages, than their patient and
calm endurance, and their steady pursuit of wealth. Hence,
though it is not impossible for a savage tribe to be Christ-
ianized, it is utterly impossible for a Christian nation to
remain a nation of savages. And not only so, but it is impossible for a Christian nation to do otherwise than constantly improve their material condition. [Whenever a
people have refused to settle down, or when settled have
refused the law of material progress, there Christianity has
found it impossible to maintain itself permanently] Not
only have the inveterate savage habits of the tribes of
America[2] repelled Christianity or ejected it from among
them, but the stereotyped barbarism of the Chinese has
been a barrier against the true faith ; and the brightest
hopes for the evangelization of India wait for their fulfilment till the abolition of Caste and the introduction of
European habits in the common affairs of life. But the
law of God is stronger than human habits; and where
habits contradictory to nature have been set against the
law of nature and the necessity of civilization, the subjects
of such habits are destined to yield and to resign the occupation of the soil. The American and Australian tribes
would seem to have been incapable of civilization ; the sub-

---

[1] Rom. xiii. and the hortatory chapters of almost every epistle.

[2] Ch. Miss. Intelligencer for March, 1854.

jects of the Jesuits in Paraguay[1] after a century and a half of settled life returned again to their woods and their wigwams; they seem to be an element which has a natural repulsion from commerce and industry. Hence the advance of Christian nations by colonies established for trade and agriculture has repelled them further and further; and like a sickly plant which has no real strength in it, they have withered away before the brightness of that light which to more vigorous organizations has proved a source of life.

We have throughout assumed the superiority of wealth and prosperity over penury and an absence of the comforts of life,—we have taken it for granted that a civilized state of existence is preferable to a savage state.[2] We trust it would be superfluous to prove this. The eulogies of Rousseau upon the state which he termed the natural state meet probably with few responses in the present day: the ideas of the origin of society with which such a view is connected belong to the age in which he lived, and have, we trust, expired with the rest of the theories of that most irreligious period. It can hardly be conceived now that men should have thought a state of ignorance better than one of enlightenment, and have desired the ultimate appeal to be to brute force rather than the moral forces which control men in a social state. It is generally admitted now that the natural state is not the most degraded but the most perfect;[3] and we need not use arguments to prove it: such arguments are weapons which have done their work, and may now rest . in their scabbards; to use them would be but to fight the

[1] Robertson's Hist. of America. The inhabitants of Peru and Mexico, having been settled nations before the Discovery of America, are the only aboriginse of America of which any large numbers have remained in a state approaching to civilization.

[2] By a savage state I understand one where the soil is not tilled nor habitations fixed. Dr. Arnold says that a barbarian nation might civilize itself; but a savage tribe could not.

[3] Remarks on certain Political Words, etc., by Cornewall Lewis. Word " Natural."

battle that is won, and to slay again the slain. /But when
the opposite view is strongly held, and it is maintained
that a state of commerce and industry is a vast improve-
ment, a thing far more *natural* than one of savage life, we
are met by the fact that commercial men have sometimes
been a curse rather than a blessing; that the rude inhabitants of the countries traded with have been degraded
not raised by contact with the traders: and further that
the very genius of commerce teaches the trader to look
solely to his own interest, disregarding the moral con-
sequences of his traffic.) The mines of Spanish America—
a very charnel-house of nations who have sickened and
died in their gloomy confinement; the plains of Mexico
and Peru with the cross raised hypocritically over scenes
of slaughter and of avarice; the coast of Africa groaning
with the loss of her sons; the Chinese slaughtered to
legalize a demoralizing though gainful trade; the tents of
western America clamorous with an unknown intoxication,
or sickening under the consequent diseases;—are these, it
is asked, the forerunners of Christianity? Are they not
rather the premonitory symptoms of desolation and death?
Nay, have not our missionaries confessed at times that the
worst evils they have had to contend against have been
the bad habits induced by contact with Europeans? And
have not the South Sea Islanders found their innocence
marred, and their pure primitive faith and habits, as
introduced by the Christian preachers, stained by the
establishment of trade?' What then can we reply? For
that these are facts, and terrible ones, cannot be denied.
We assert that they are exceptions; that they are not
necessary parts of the advance of civilization; that so far
from being done in the interests of commerce they are in
direct contradiction to its best and highest laws,—deeds

' Bp. Armstrong, the new Bp. of Graham's Town, stated at a public meet-
ing that the prejudice of the nations against Europeans was likely to prove
his most serious opponent.—See Article of Qu. Review before alluded to.
See also Narrative of a visit to the Consular cities of China, by G. Smith,
now. Bp. of Victoria.

done for the immediate and selfish gain of individuals engaged in it, but abhorent to its truest interests. We turn to a comparison between the civilized nations and barbarous tribes, and declare that the state of the one excels that of the other as far as the light excels the darkness; and we desire that all may participate in the benefits which belong to the most enlightened. If, in the process of change, evils occur, which we cannot foresee, because they form no necessary part of a change which is purely good in its design, but arise from the evil motives of those who are employed in effecting that change, the evil must be laid upon the perpetrators of it; it is not fairly changeable upon commerce or upon civilization. We may turn from such scenes as we have described to sights of a more pleasing character—to Borneo pacified and settled and reduced to law by a commercial nation'—to India governed paternally and justly by a joint stock company.—We may take the objector to the coast of Africa, and while he enumerates its wrongs and makes us weep for its past history, we may point him to desolations repaired, to wildernesses cultivated—to a population once designed for slavery now taught by the welcomed missionary, and flourishing under the blessings of a legitimate commerce.

Commerce then, is always beneficial in its general results, and therefore it is sanctioned by Christianity/ But it by no means follows that the commercial spirit is a Christian one. A good object is not always brought about by good men—often men's worst motives are overruled for good, and the contending passions of individuals made subservient to the good of mankind. When we speak, therefore, of the commercial spirit, as we shall do further on, we must expect to find, that, however good commerce itself may be in its general benefits to our race, it has much of selfishness mixed up with it, and partakes of that stain which vitiates all that is human.

And here we may close our first inquiry. The con-

---

¹ Sir J. Brookes Letters have recently been published.

elusion at which we arrive is this: That commerce is a general good, and sanctioned by Christianity; that it has usually paved the way for the advance of the true religion; that though that religion may have advanced at times beyond its sphere, commerce has come in as an auxiliary and a support; and that, where this support has been wanting or has been refused, Christianity has turned away from a disobedient race and migrated to a more hospitable region.

II. We may now proceed to our second inquiry; the influence of commerce upon the doctrines and practice of Christianity.

And first we may observe that Christianity, which reveals to us super-sensible things, is yet under the necessity of teaching them by means of sensible images and of words borrowed from daily life: also, that, when these ideas have been so conveyed to our minds, we are still under the necessity of conceiving of them through the medium of the images given us, and of arguing about them by analogies. Hence the greater part of the teaching of the New Testament is contained in direct parables, or in comparisons, and symbols, and metaphors; and by this parabolical method we find all the common pursuits of mankind interwoven with our conceptions of the highest truths. Commerce, as one of these pursuits, and one of the most common, is constantly used to represent the dealings of God with man, and phrases borrowed from commercial language are closely wrought in with the doctrines of our faith. God is the landlord, who lets out his vineyard to husbandmen;[1] God is the master who pays the labourers an exact sum for their work;[2] the fruition of Christ is a treasure hid in a field,[3] or a pearl, to buy which we give up all our other merchandize;—our worldly possessions are pieces of money which we are to trade with for our master.[4] The saints are bought with a price,[5]

---

[1] Matt. xxi. 33.   [2] Matt. xx. 1.   [3] Matt. xiii. 5.   [4] Luke xix. 13.
[5] 1 Cor. vi. 20., vii. 23.

and their state of glory is an inheritance which is pur-
chased for them.[1] Such as these are the analogies presented to us to convey the ideas of God's dealings with
us. But we must bear in mind that they are only analogies, and that an argument from analogy must not be
pressed too far. In all similar things there are elements
of dissimilarity, and often it is but a single point in which
there is a comparison. To argue therefore from all the
parts of the symbol to all the parts of the thing symbolized
must be erroneous. Yet such modes of argument have constantly been used in Theology, and often with most per-
nicious results.

The liability to error is here greatly increased by an im-
perfect notion of justice. The commercial transactions
between man and man are the most simple and palpable instances in which the principles of justice are exemplified :
here right and wrong, falsehood and truth, are most easily
detected. But they are by no means the only instances ;
and to take them as the universal representations—to borrow
our ideas of Justice exclusively from them, must lead us
into error. This error Aristotle fell into[2] when he represented the injury done by one man to another as merely so
much loss and gain to the respective parties, which might
be righted like the scales of a balance Such a represen-
tation gives us no proper notion of the sanctity of law
or the binding obligations of morality. If then this be the
case in the transactions between man and man—if we are
conscious that a higher notion than that of commercial ex-
change ought to enter into them—how inadequate must
such notions of barter be to express the obligations and
dealings of man with his Creator. When therefore such

---

[1] Eph. i. 14.

Many commercial metaphors are used—the Scripture both Old and New
Testament. Thus in Dan. v. 27. " Thou art weighed in the balances and
found wanting."

[2] Arist. Eth. Nic. в. v.—his word for dealings (συναλλάγματα) includes
both commercial bargains and cases such as theft, assault, etc.

notions are used in Scripture, we must be careful to remember that they are but analogies, the images of things, not the things themselves. God is represented to us as entering into an agreement with man and swearing to that agreement—man as breaking that agreement and incurring the predetermined fine—Christ as paying the debt for him. And these analogies hold good as representing to us that God demands a perfect obedience, that man has by disobedience incurred the wrath of God, and that Christ has brought about a reconciliation. But men who have not been willing to be satisfied with the grand revelations which God has made, but would pry into the means and reasons of His dealings, have endeavoured to define what He has not defined—to comprehend the incomprehensible. Having therefore the symbol or type before them, they have argued the correspondence of all the parts of the typified scheme with the parts of the scheme used as a type. Hence have arisen views and speculations on the divine dealings as frivolous as they are distasteful. The sacrifice of Christ has been looked upon as an exact sum to be weighed against the sins of mankind, or a price exactly equivalent to the debt that was owed; or, by those who limit Redemption, as just sufficient to redeem the souls of the elect. Or, again, the merits and righteousness of Christ have been supposed to be a treasury full of coin, or to be minutely subdivisible into fractions exactly corresponding to particular sins. Again, the sins of men have been looked upon as exactly valuable at a certain price, as a certain sum of honour or respect taken away from the Almighty, and hence has followed that distinction of venial and mortal sins so fatal not only to all sound theology but also to morality. Again, in connection with the doctrine of purgatory,[1] it has been supposed that a certain amount of torment and suffering might be remitted in consideration of an equivalent in merit, and thus a debtor and creditor account was kept,

---

[1] Perhaps the doctrine of purgatory itself may be traced to the commercial language which is used; it goes upon the supposition that the suffering endure is a repayment on the part of the sufferer equivalent to certain offences.

which could actually be represented by the coin, in which masses and liturgies were paid for⌋ ⌊It was against the last of these errors that Luther's wrath was aroused, and that protest uttered which shook the world⌋ And surely we may well echo that protest, not only against that particular form of the error, but against all such attempts to limit God's dealings and to bind the Infinite within the rules and technicalities of human exchanges.

Such are some of the effects which commercial language has had upon Christian doctrine; effects in the terminology of Theology in the first instance, and afterwards upon teaching and upon practice. We have now to consider the effect of the commercial spirit on those classes and states and individuals where it has mostly flourished, and how it has influenced their views and conduct as regards Christianity. In this consideration we shall have to speak of commerce chiefly as modifying the views and characters of men and of Christianity as manifesting itself in schemes and theories and polities. What then is the influence generally of commerce upon the views the feelings and the character of those who engage in it?

⌊The pursuits of commerce are essentially individualizing.⌋ The merchant has but one principal end in all his undertakings, and that end is his own advantage. He contributes, no doubt, in a high degree to the good of society; but this is not his object as a merchant. To the merchant the welfare of society is quite a secondary consideration.[1] Nor would the most enlightened view of the benefits of commerce to society teach him to act otherwise, than with a view to his own interests. The philanthropic and charitable merchant who should in a time of scarcity sell his bread to the poor at a lower rate than the market price, would but cause a momentary abundance and

---

[1] We must bear in mind the distinction drawn in p. 17 between the general results of commerce (which are always beneficial) and the objects with which each man engages in it. This is a necessary distinction in the case of all professions: the aim of a system of law is justice to all, but the aim of any single lawyer may be simply his own advantage.

cheapness, to be followed by a still greater scarcity; and his effort of generosity would do harm rather than good. But it does not require any such consideration as this to induce the generality of men to seek their own interests above all things, and a trader needs not usually to be reminded not to be quixotic or over generous in his bargains. Thus the merchant's views terminate in himself; however vast his schemes, however long the vista of his speculations, he himself stands reflected at the end of them all; his ideal state has but one prominent figure, and that figure is himself, He is the centre of all, and the other beings who live and move around him are in magnitude before his mental vision proportioned to their bearing upon and relation to himself. He mixes with society—society is to pay him for his wares. He is a member of a state—that state is to protect his life and his property. His pursuits necessarily connect him with a hundred different persons, and often with as many countries; and his views reach over oceans, and he has ties which bind him to the antipodes; and he may be affected for good or for evil by persons or by circumstances at the remotest limits of the earth. But he is conscious that he is his own master, that he can sever himself at any moment from his schemes and his business, that he sits loosely to all his ties, and can change and modify his circumstances at will. He can dispose of his trade to another man, he can sell his ships or his factory; and turning from the anxieties and intricacies of commercial life he can retire into the simple and peaceful security of the fund-holder. ⌊He alone in the midst of his ties and his circumstances is independent and self-sufficient. He owns no allegiance to any man or any country⌋ He is a frequenter of all lands, but a citizen of none; and the merchant-prince is but a world-wide adventurer. Were it not that his mode of existence is less ethereal, and the substance on which he lives more material and palpable, we might compare him to the orchideous plant which owns not itself indebted to the earth for its subsistence, but spreads forth its roots into the air, and draws its vital sap from the open light and pure breath of the heavens.

In such a character as this there are many principles far from attractive. Let us examine them a little more minutely. The most notable of them is pride: but this does not belong to commercial men peculiarly; it has a universal grasp of the mind of fallen men, from which no human power can free us. For wherein does pride consist? It is that very self-reflecting tendency, which turns the eye of an intellectual creature inwardly upon himself, and induces him to look upon his own character with self-complacent delight; and this it is which existing in the heart of man is the very source and fountain of that corruption which Christianity is designed to conquer. Arising from a false feeling of independence, a want of trust in the Almighty Being who gave him breath, it has alienated man from his Creator, and consequently from his brethren. But among men as social beings there is a counteracting tendency in the felt and acknowledged dependence of man on man, which to a certain extent restores the confidence which has been lost, leading us to look forth out of ourselves, and feel that we are not alone, that we are not the greatest and most worthy of all things in the universe, that we are men and not gods. Now the commercial spirit, as fostering the self-sufficient and self-asserting tendency in our nature, or at least by loosening the ties which bind us to our fellow men, seems to have a direct tendency to increase the principle of pride by diminishing its natural antidote. The merchant-prince,[1] as he looks out upon the world and thinks of it in its relation to himself, makes himself, as it were, the centre of the universe: and as he reflects upon his wealth, a possession which all nations respect,—of his power and sovereignty attested by ships in every ocean and by multitudes dependent upon him for the supplies of daily life—of his complete independence and self-sufficiency, which can say to his

[1] See the character of Sidonia in Disraeli's Coningsby.

fellows, I have no need of you, and to friendships and supports which common men lean upon, I am beyond and above your influence,—as he reflects upon these, like the monarch in his imperial city, his heart will be lifted up with the thought of his own magnificence, and the humbler and kindlier feelings of our nature be banished or at least obscured. The spirit which said, "Is not this great Babylon which I have builded," was not that which breathed "Little children love one another."

Again, in the practical business of life, in the bustling, crowded thoroughfare, in the desperate eagerness of speculation, or the sharp encounter of competition, there is little room for the play of the finer social feelings. There is but one side of human nature which a life spent in such affairs as these brings out, and that by no means the most agreeable side. It was said by Phocylides [1] that when a man was rich he should begin to practice virtue; we may say with more truth, that till a man has some leisure from the perpetual whirl of commercial pursuits, he cannot attend to the refinement of a polished and highly wrought state of society. His attention is confined to what is useful in morals, and he has no leisure for the beautiful. Quickness of perception, soundness of judgment, promptness of determination, energy of execution, a single eye to his own interests, and to the object before him,—caution, and secrecy, and reserve—these and other similar qualities are brought out and intensified to their highest power; and he will be truthful and conscientious, upright and manly and straight-forward in his dealings. But as he passes along through the thoroughfare of the world, pushing his own way and jostling those who oppose themselves—as he rushes along the road with his eye fixed upon a single object and without a glance at the fair landscape on either hand,—will he not become hard, and rough, and unimpressible? Will not the tenderer fibres of the texture of his moral nature be rudely torn, and the light down which

[1] Plato's Republic, b. III.

adorned it be worn off, and the keen sensibilities of his
nervous framework be rendered callous by the shocks and
impact of external violence?

Again, it must be admitted that the pursuits of commerce
do not necessitate a high degree of intellectual culture, nor
require a fine taste or a nice discrimination. Hence there is
a danger of a certain vulgarity and coarseness of apprehen-
sion in the handling of intellectual matters or of things in
which an acuteness and refinement of mental perception is
required. A certain roughness of judgment, a too broad
and general classification of things, a want of patient and
minute consideration of views differing from his own, and
a difficulty or unwillingness to appreciate the complexity
of motives or the delicate sensibility by which so many
sincere persons are led—these are often the results of an
all-engrossing pursuit which draws the mind into a channel
by no means deep enough for its full developement, and
yet affords sufficient scope in point of extent and surface
for its constant and assiduous employment.

Yet when the worst has been said that can be said of the
demerits of the commercial character, there is nothing to
prove it hostile to Christianity·which may not be equalled
or even surpassed in any of the other pursuits of life ; nothing, indeed, which could overthrow a claim, were such a
claim set up for it, to be the most conducive and the most
adaptable of all pursuits to a right reception of the Christian religion. It may be that some of the qualities which
we have described as characteristic of the commercial
spirit, may seem, as described, to be hostile to the spirit of
Christianity ; but this is the result mostly of excess or mis-
direction : and each of the principles, which are so fre-
quently modified by evil, are perfectly capable of being
modified by good. If the commercial man is single-minded in his selfishness, he may also be single-minded in his
benevolence : if his talents are adapted to the carrying out
simply and earnestly of ends which terminate in himself,
they are fit also for carrying out ends which terminate in
the good of others. That he sits loosely to the cares of

social and political life may but render him more efficient
in schemes of universal philanthropy; his carelessness of
minor and subsidiary ends make him all the more able to
concentrate his energies upon the grandest and noblest;
and his indifference to subtleties make him perceive more
distinctly and grasp more firmly, the grand principles
which are the foundation alike of Christian doctrine and
practice. And there is a class of virtues which are especially bound up with commercial dealings and directly
fostered by them.[1] Integrity and uprightness, a scrupulous
truthfulness, a generous confidence and a noble self-respect,
are qualities which trade directly tends to produce, and
which give a moral dignity to the commercial character
which when sanctified by Christianity may bear comparison
with any type of human nature. We are not, however,
concerned with the comparative excellence of commerce
and other pursuits, but with the influence, which, as a
matter of history, commerce has had upon Christianity.
It may be, it probably is the case, that, as far as the
acceptance of vital Christianity is concerned, one pursuit
presents nearly as many obstacles as another. Generally
speaking, the opposition to Christianity lies far deeper
than the influences of any occupation can reach, and religion, to make any impression, must deal with the deep
source, not with the stream as it flows, or the channel into
which it runs. But, though the reception of Christianity
may not be prevented or induced by the external circumstances in which a man is placed, these circumstances may
have great power in the working out and assimilation of
particular parts of the Christian scheme. It is the glory
of Christianity that it is not a religion of one clime or of
one race or one class, but adapted to all alike; but while
addressing itself to all men equally, the forms and manner
of its manifestation are infinitely diversified. It contains
a scheme for satisfying the spiritual wants of mankind,

---

[1] See Dr. Chalmers's Commercial Sermons, especially that on the Commercial Virtues.

accounting to them for the contradictions existing in their
nature, and solving the problems of sin and righteousness
and judgment which have perplexed them : it also contains
a rule of life and a definite sanction for morals. And in
both these parts it is susceptable of infinite modifications.
Whether, if all Christian men could be perfected as Christians, there would still remain that diversity of view which
is apparent now among men who yet in the truest sense
are Christians, may well be doubted : that they would not
be alike in their modes of thought, or the method of their
lives, we may take for granted ; for this, were it the case
would destroy all independence. But, however this may
be, it is certain that many different forms of Christianity
are presented to us in the world, and that these forms are
in many cases influenced by, if not directly traceable to,
the pursuits and habits of those in whom they are manifested. Is the influence of commerce, then, to be traced in
the views of Christianity adopted by men and communities
of the commercial class ? Is there any view or system of
Christianity which corresponds to and is connected with
the principles of the commercial spirit ? We think there
certainly is ; and to bring out the connection, we may
sketch broadly the two grand divisions of Christian opinion,
arising from the prominence respectively of certain elements in the human mind, and from two distinct types of
human character.

The one of these looks upon Christianity as a system, a
polity, with an external and visible aspect, but with a
power over the unseen and the spiritual : it leads a man to
throw himself into such a system, to submit to its laws, to
trust to its ordinances and rules, and to be led and incited
and even compelled by them into a complete submission to
the will of God and a compliance with those spiritual conditions which are laid down for our performance in the
charter of the Divine covenant. It looks upon the church
as a divinely appointed agency for bringing men into acceptance with God, and considers all who are willing to
profess Christianity as members of that church. The

Church is the grand instructress, who is to educate her children for Christ. Under this general description will be undoubtedly included many diversities of opinion, diversities which to some men may seem the capital and fundamental distinctions. But, as in one sense all truth is one and all error is opposition to or denial of the truth, so we are bound to admit that all truly Christian men have been one in the most essential matters; and since in both the great divisions of opinion which we are establishing there are truly Christian men, the greatest and supremest distinction between man and man remains still untouched; our division is more one of opinion and of form than of fundamental disposition. Both views have somewhat of truth in them; both may be grievously perverted. Thus the view already spoken of will include among its supporters those who,[1] seeing the power of social opinion, look on the Church as a divinely appointed instrument to bring them to Christ; but it will include also those who hold the sacerdotal principle and make the priest a necessary mediator between the Christian and his Lord.

The other view of Christianity looks upon man in his independence and individuality, standing alone and naked in the presence of his Maker, where no human support can avail him, nor any thought intrude, whether as intervening or as accessory, but that of his own responsibility before the heart-searching gaze of his Judge. It was this grand aspect of Theology which the Reformers brought so prominently into view, and which in their eyes and those of their successors so completely outshone the minor and lower considerations, as to put all systems and accessory helps completely out of sight. It asserts continually the futility of all that is human, the insufficiency of external supports, the destructive error of trusting to priests or to churches, the necessity of personal repentance, and of a per-

---

[1] See Arnold's fragment on the Church; also his inaugural lecture on Mod. Hist. His theory of co-operation presumes that each member of the Church is willing to co-operate. But the mass of men in a Christian country refuse to submit to spiritual Christianity.

sonal relationship with God, felt and acknowledged; the importance of sincerity and self-judgment; the singleness and simplicity of that faith, which each man must for himself possess or be for ever without the blessings which faith secures. Hence the whole direction of its teaching has the one aim of bringing the truth to bear upon individuals; it leaves the propagation of that truth to individual exertion; it looks upon the Church as an invisible collection of individual believers, and makes Christian communion to consist in reciprocity of sentiment among such believers fortuitously congregated together. It is this latter view of Christianity which has in it the elements fitted to combine with the commercial spirit. That tendency which segregates and isolates a man in his own view from those among whom he lives, which constantly insists upon his independence and self-sufficiency, has a natural connection with a religious system which takes a man simply as an individual, and tells him of his own unaided responsibility: and the same habit of mind which in the business of life looks constantly to a single aim, impatiently disregarding all minor conveniences, that sober, calculating spirit, which looks at the end proposed and considers nothing else but how that end may be attained, will in religion look simply to the one grand object, and while that is secure, will mind little besides.

But if the abstract coincidence of the two things be admitted—if it has been proved that in the nature of things there is something in the commercial spirit which inclines a man to the independent and individual view of Christianity, much more is this connection manifested when we descend into the lower sphere, the sphere of concrete things, politics, and history, and ecclesiastical matters. The view of Christianity which we first spoke of, has generally brought forth fruit in the shape of hierarchies and sacerdotal systems, which in spiritual matters have pretended to intervene between man and God, and in practical matters have set up a tyranny over opinions and over actions. With its confessionals and directions, its ceremonies and pageant, its enforcement of external obedience, its outward, verbal assurances of condemnation or forgiveness, and its viaticum ministered by the priest, it has presented what the superstitious have been too ready to accept, a prop to support them and give them hope, an external and perfunctory way of salvation. It has opposed itself to free enquiry and unfettered judgment, has leagued itself with tyranny in the political world, and by setting up its throne in the most vital and essential part of human nature, has aspired to universal dominion. Such an ecclesiastical system has, through the sluggishness and inertness of mankind, held sway at most times and in most places; but among the bright spots, where the truth has burst through this bondage none have been more conspicuous than those where the commercial spirit has been its supporter. The pursuits of agriculture in which men have been habituated to a graduated scale of society and have in this manner imbibed a spirit of dependence and even of servility, have been found fitted for the habitation and developement of such a system; and still more so has the regular discipline and organization of an army. But commerce has always rebelled against it and fretted at the bit which curbed its liberty. The man who was not attached to the soil, but looked abroad over oceans for the means of his subsistence, who became acquainted with other states and other institutions than those of his fatherland, could not be bound down by systems and rules like those whose views were bounded by the place of their own abode, who had never breathed the free air of ocean nor felt themselves citizens of the world. This man is independent; who shall prescribe his actions or form a channel for his opinions? He is versatile and possessed of powers which may be turned to a thousand objects; who shall presume to direct their application? He may admit your principles, but you cannot bind him with your rules. You may exert a moral influence over him, but to fetter him in his particular actions—no man has power for that. You may depress him and weigh him down, but there is an elasticity in

him which will recoil upon yourself; or, if you think to
force him and secure his submission, at the moment when
you have hedged him round and made his house a very
prison to him, he may on a sudden gather round him his
wealth and property and be gone across the seas, where
the arm of your power may reach after him in vain.

It is by no means meant to assert that it is impossible
to find a scheme, moderate, comprehensive, and philo-
sophical, which should give the advantages of system
without losing those of individuality; nor to maintain
that the independent spirit has always been in the right,
never violating order nor running into eccentricities. But,
as a matter of fact, the world has witnessed the ecclesiastical system in its most extravagant and erroneous form,
and the spirit which in such cases has opposed it, has, even
when purely negative and revolutionary, been beneficial.
So great a debt do we owe to commerce as the uncompro-
mising antagonist of the sacerdotal principle. The two
things cannot long abide together; the one or the other
must give way. The Danes and the Dutch, the English
on both sides of the Atlantic, are witnesses of this principle.
Their commerce has expelled the priestly system and
resisted its introduction again and again. The Reforma-
tion persecuted in France was harboured and supported
for awhile in La Rochelle and Lyons; and when driven
out of their country the French Protestants found refuge
in England and the Netherlands. In Germany no stronger
resistance was opposed to the great back-wave of Catholicism
under Charles V. than that which was offered by the
cities of the Hanseatic league;[1] and of the dominions of
Philip II. the only part which preserved independence of
religion or of government were the Dutch merchants
under the Prince of Orange.[2] Spain and Portugal on
the other hand whose commerce was once in the van

---

[1] See Robertson's Hist. of Charles V, B. ix, x. At one time even these cities
were compelled to submit to the Interim.

[2] See Smyth's Lect. on Mod. Hist. Lect. 12.

of all the nations,[1] and might, in connection with their
colonies, have continued to flourish and to be a blessing
to their population, yielded to the power of tyranny and
and priestly domination; their melancholy condition in
the present day, their total stagnation during nearly three
centuries, is a sad proof of what ecclesiastical tyranny and
the prohibition of free thought may effect. They bowed
their heads to the yoke, and the yoke has weighed them
down; they kept their superstition, but their commerce
and their energy vanished.[2] An instance more particular
of the brighter side of the picture may be found in the
contrast between the Anglo-Saxon race in England and in
America. There, across the Atlantic, we have a purely
commercial and industrial community, speculators, money
makers and traders, a democracy such as the world has
never seen: and in harmony with the levelling and equal-
izing tone of opinion in political and social life, we find a
purely independent spirit in ecclesiastical matters. The
religious institutions of the United States are entirely regulated by the laws of commerce, the rules of supply and
demand. In England on the other hand we have a two-
fold element, both in church and state, a great aristocracy
and a still greater industrial system, and these are manifested both in the social and religious sentiment of the people. The character of the English is swayed by both the
aristocratical and the industrial spirit; it alternates between
a respect for aristocratic principles, feelings and manners,
and a democratic tendency to level all ranks in a great
industrial state. Corresponding with this alternation of
social feeling, we have two systems of ecclesiastical politics working side by side together. The Church of England is the church of the aristocracy and of those who
either aspire to aristocracy in some shape or hold to the
ancient state of things from a conservative spirit. But the

[1] Robertson's Hist. of America.

[2] The trading communities of Italy in the middle ages had not the choice
of two religions; but they constantly resisted the authority of the Pope and
the ecclesiastics.

mechanic and the tradesman prefers the Chapel; he loves to feel that he is on a level with those among whom he worships, and to pay for his spiritual as for his bodily wants according to the rules of commerce. Even in the internal constitution of the church of England we may observe the double principle, for the church is not altogether aristocratic; the orderly and systematic element, the more refined and elegant tendency, which looks at once to the permanent, the symmetrical and the beautiful, is represented by our bishops and our endowments, our cathedrals and our ordered liturgy. That commercial and democratic spirit on the other hand which looks only to the convenient and the useful, which makes institutions according to its needs and leaves to posterity the option of keeping or of discontinuing them, manifests itself in the pew-rents and propietary chapels of our larger towns and in the chuch-rates, and vestries, and in the independent attitude of our great religious societies.

Thus then we may close our second inquiry in which (1.) we have observed the effects of commercial language and thoughts upon views of religious doctrine (2.) we have traced a connection between the independent character of the commercial mind and an independent system of religious belief; and (3.) following out this connection into a lower sphere, we have remarked the choice of democratic institutions in matters of church government and the opposition to spiritual tyranny which has constantly been made by those classes and nations who have been freed by the enlarging influence of the commercial spirit.

We have looked into the past and spoken of its history; may we not say a word as to the future? We have gathered tendencies and principles: but what are our feelings and our hopes? In the last half-century there has sprung up a spirit of invention and of enterprise unknown before; and commerce till lately comparatively inert, is springing and running and flying with a more rapid motion of every limb, no longer dependent on the slowness of road-travelling or the fitfulness of breezes, but self-propelled by the

living and roaring leviathan within her bosom. The black
lines of rails, which as an iron bond consolidate into one
the civilized world; the light cords of the telegraph which
speak for us through the air and through the earth and
through the sea, then tell us of the mighty commercial
energy in the midst of which we live. Our land is rat-
tling with the spinning jenny and the shuttle, and even
the slow motions of a rustic population are quickened, as
they wonder at the engine that thrashes their corn and
admire the fresh comforts and conveniences which each
new invention places within their reach. In truth the
world seems living faster than of old: the pulse of human
nature is beating and throbbing with a more rapid movement. The population of England has doubled itself within
fifty years, and mighty towns have arisen, where but lately
were fields and marshes. And as we look forth into the
world we see new nations arising, new fields of commerce
opening. The barbarous New Holland of 1800 became
the civilized community of Australia by 1850—The isth-
mus of Darien about to be cut through, and two oceans
joined into one—gold in Australia—gold in California—
China opening her ports to trade after thousands of years
of exclusion, and a decayed race in the east of Europe
reviving under the united influence of an ancient faith
and a novel commerce.[1] It is emphatically the age of
trade and industry. We have celebrated the festival of
material civilization in the great Exhibition of the nations'
industry, and called all ends of the earth to unite with us
in the triumph of patient and laborious progress. It was
a noticeable fact, that in a bay of that Exhibition was a
stand of books laid open to all readers; they were spread
out wide to attract the gaze of those who should pass by.
It was the Book, the Word of God, the revelation of
Christianity, published in more than a hundred languages

---

[1] The Greeks have now all the carrying-trade of the Levant in their hands;
they trade also extensively with other countries, and have factories and even
churches in England.

of the nations of the earth. That fact is not a solitary or an isolated one; for coeval with the advance of commerce and of practical science, there has taken place a mighty advance of Christianity. More has been done for the cause of the Gospel in the last fifty years, than in any similar period since the days of the Apostles. We have seen in that time a new religious impulse, a new effort to evangelize the earth; we have seen in our own country congregations collected and churches built where there were none before,[1] and societies founded for Christian purposes of every description, and rival sects, whose zeal, though, alas, often directed against each others' bosoms, has yet, in the main, advanced the cause of a living and a true religion. We see the mission work giving unquestionable symptoms of vitality, of real solid fruit, such as none who interest themselves in the cause can deny; we see under its influence a general movement after good, — the savage turned from his cannibalism and his fetish to peace and industry, and submission to the faith of Christ,—the slave trade conquered after a battle of forty years; we see China shaking herself loose from a retrograde and debasing system, beginning to profess Christianity and to welcome Christian nations,[2]—India relaxing the inequalities of her castes beneath the joint efforts of commercial and Christian enlightenment. In the east the crescent is waning, and a purer faith begins to dawn among the valleys of Palestine;[3] and in Europe even the nations held

---

[1] The difference of population and church accommodation in the years 1801 and 1851 is given in the Report of Religious Worship recently published, as follows :—1801, pop. 8,829,536, accom. 5,171,123 ;—1851, pop. 17-927.609. accom. 9,212,563.

[2] See a letter of the Bishop of Victoria in Ch. Miss. Intelligencer of August, 1853. Also "China her Future and her Past;" a charge to the Anglican Clergy, delivered in Trinity Church, Shanghae, October 20th, 1853. The Bishop seems to have more hopes of the religion of the rebels than have generally been entertained in England. But however this may be great benefits will be gained if the exclusive system be completely overthrown.

[3] An edict of toleration was issued by the sultan a few years ago to protect the infant communities of Protestants.

down by priestly tyranny, are bestirring themselves
beneath their chains, and talking of liberty and free
opinion. And what is, then, the end to which we are
tending? Alas we have but begun. How little a way
have we made in the march of civilization; how small a
portion of our ideal picture of Christian optimism have we
as yet filled up. After forty years of peace the de-
mon of war is again amongst us. Vice and infidelity
swarm in the midst of us ;[1] the cause of education lan-
guishes ; the most Christian nations are but tinged
with Christianity ; the most wealthy do but stave
off the gnawing penury which breaks in at every
cessation of effort. Truly, now, as of old, the creation
groans and travails. In the midst of this depression,
this corruption of nature, who is there that has the
courage to raise his head and not despair? who, to believe
the promise that the kingdoms of this world shall become
the kingdoms of God? It may be that theories of human
progress are rash and enthusiastic, the product of youthful
imagination. Be it so: the world has suffered more from
its inertness than its enthusiasm; and the cause of its sloth
is its abandonment of hope. But if we maintain our hope,
in what does that hope consist? Is it merely the hope of
each individual for his own deliverance? Is there no
promise to the world at large, to society, to the whole
creation? It may not be, it is not true, that the individual is lost and absorbed in the wave of social progress,
that we

" linger on the shore,[2]
And the individual withers, and the world is more and more."

But neither is it true that the world is lost in the man,
that hope is to be confined to the extrication of the individual from a world that is corrupt and perishing. That
same faith which teaches us to have hope for ourselves in

---

[1] See Report of Religious Worship. Also two Essays on Juvenile Deprav-
ity, published for a Prize 1848.

[2] Tennyson's Locksley Hall.

a crucified Saviour, tells us that that Saviour is the first-born of a new creation :[1] the groan in which both man and nature combine has in it a promise for both together, an assurance that the creation too shall be delivered from its bondage.[2] The Redeemer spoke not only of deliverance, but also of regeneration ;[3] and the last words he left us tell us that the time comes quickly when he shall say "Behold I make all things new." The toil of human bodies and human souls, the throes of a suffering world are not without an object. They are the efforts after a higher and a better condition, not mere graspings after selfish gratification. Do we ask what is the good of our striving,[4] when we have the promise of a regeneration? Why we should work, when God has said that He will work? Surely such questionings are the essence of un-belief. We cannot see far into the future; but in the darkness a gleam of light meets us from on high, a gleam of hope and of promise. We know not how that promise is to be fulfilled, but we believe in Him who gave it us. We see even in this state of weakness certain incipient elements of strength, in this prevailing sorrow certain things which bring us joy. We know that the misery of mankind is relieved by social comfort and civilization—that a thousand temptations to evil fostered by distress are re-moved by material plenty; and that there is a bond between the moral and physical world so strongly bound that we cannot strive against evil in the one without striving against it in the other also. We are taught, further, that the origin of both [5] moral and physical evil is identical, and that the remover of the one is the remover of the other also. While therefore, we deem it an aimless and a useless task to labour without faith, and luxury unaccompanied

---

[1] Πρωτότοκος πάσης κτίσεως.—Col. i. 15.

[2] Romans viii.   [3] Matt. xix. 25.

[4] This appears to have been the notion of the Thessalonians, which St. Paul reproved in his 2nd Epistle to them ; but their cessation of labour arose from a mistaken faith not from unbelief.

[5] Cursed is the ground for thy sake. Gen. iii. 17.

by the love of God is but the stalled ox with enmity, we acknowledge cheerfully the connection of the blessing with our own exertions. We take comfort from the promise of revelation, but we use the natural instruments placed in our hands, and trust to the law of Providence as well as to the law of Grace, and hail the progress of all that relieves the wants of man, that tends to make his condition happier, and bring the smile of joy over the downcast human countenance, not as something trivial and fleeting and accidental, but a very foretaste of the day when God shall wipe away tears from every face.

But if indeed we may look for a brighter era, for a fulfilment of our highest hopes, and the world is advancing gradually but surely according to the purposes of God— how grand, how commanding is the position of the Anglo-Saxon race in reference to such a progression. We have occupied some of the fairest regions of the globe : upon our dominion the sun sets not ; our commerce is in every sea, our missionaries in all the ocean's isles. We have a goodly heritage, and we know how to value religion and liberty and commerce. We are rich and powerful, laborious and energetic, with a character for honesty and uprightness which is the source of a mighty influence, and with a will to perform that which we have purposed. Let us hold fast that we have : let it grow and become stronger and stronger. Confidently and trustfully let us look to the future—anxiously let us purge out the evil that is amongst us,—laboriously let us pursue the duties of our position. Let the faith of a crucified Christ be the hope of our nation—the faith of One who toiled and suffered and now is glorified. And let us be to the world an example that His kingdom comes not by a denial of evil, nor by a passive inertness under its dominion ; but by admitting the evil, and accepting the remedy ; by a humble obedience to the laws both of Revelation and of nature, of faith and also of Industry ; and by maintaining our confidence assured, that in so doing the day will break around us and the desire of the nations be accomplished.

SYNOPSIS.

OXFORD:
PRINTED BY MORRIS AND BURROUGH,
HIGH STREET.

CPSIA information can be obtained
at www.ICGtesting.com
Printed in the USA
BVHW041120150119
537879BV00009B/151/P